NEANDERTHAL MAN LOVES TREE HUGGER

Neanderthal Man is a 40-something, ex-British soldier who collects exotic knives and can strip down a semi-automatic rifle blind-folded. Until recently, he thought 'chakras' was a Latina pop star whose hips don't lie. But things changed for the card-carrying caveman when he met the Tree Hugger. He survived combat and guard duty but will he survive crystal healing workshops and green smoothies?

By
Tamara Pitelen & Adrian Maul

First edition: 2015
Updated edition 2: 2017
Updated edition 3: 2019

ISBN-13: 978-1-9160116-1-8

Blue Dea Books

DEDICATION

To Anne, Janet, Rick and David. We love you. We thank you.

4

CONTENTS

CHAPTER ONE

PAPER UNDIES AND MASSAGE FOR MEN

Massage, so what's that all about then? What's with the poncy oils and rainforest music? Back when I was in the army, we were always getting injured and being packed off to the physiotherapist but I don't remember any candles or Buddha statues.

The only experience I'd had of massage was one of them free head and shoulder rubs they give you in the Etihad business class airport lounge. For me, these were all about killing time till my flight was called. Nice enough if they were free but I couldn't understand why anyone would pay good money to be rubbed in smelly oil for an hour with whale music playing in the background.

Then, earlier this year, I had my first proper massage. I was on holiday at Six Senses Zighy Bay on the Musandam Peninsula in Oman with the Tree Hugger – she's no stranger to the kind of pampering that involves being plastered in exotic oils, scrubs and seaweed wraps so I decided to see what it was all about and booked a 60 minute Oriental massage.

"Would you prefer a man or a woman," they asked. That threw me. Does it matter? Is that a trick question? Is there a wrong answer?

"Umm… not bothered," I mumbled so I got a man. That's when it dawned on me; I was paying a man to touch me!

Paying. A. Man. To. TOUCH. Me! With his hands!

The last man who touched my body in an intimate way was the doctor who slapped me on the backside when I was born. I felt nausea rising.

It got worse. I was given a robe, towel, flip flops and disposable underpants to put on. Disposable underpants?! What on earth were paper undies for? How did I end up almost naked in this alien land where grown men pay other grown men to 'touch' them? I say 'touch' but it soon transpired that this kind of touching was really painful. On discovering that my back was a landscape of concrete rocks, the therapist set to work, vigorously rubbing, kneading, pulling, pressing... it was like hot knives being pushed into my shoulders. Still, amidst the agony, my paranoid mind kept throwing up the irrational fear that this man – who was half my size by the way – would leap on me at any minute with a view to molestation.

He didn't of course, and afterwards I felt pretty good yet bruised.

A month or so later, me and the Tree Hugger were in Thailand. Again, I found myself getting dragged off for a massage. This was the kind where they only do your feet. There's a special word for it, 'reflexology'. It was big news to me that every part of your body is represented on the soles of your feet – not sure I believe that my sinuses are going to be cleared by rubbing my toes though. Again, there was a bit of pain but afterwards I realised that my previously very tired feet were completely rejuvenated. I was starting to get the point of all this massage stuff.

I am now sold on the concept of regular massage. The way I see it, the human body is like a high performance car that requires ongoing maintenance to keep it in tip top condition, like a service every 10,000km. I still haven't completely accepted the thing about paying a man to touch me but I'm getting there.

CHAPTER TWO

MALE BONDING AND BEDROOM ISSUES

"Oh go on Honey, it's a great chance for some honest male bonding!" burbled the Tree Hugger as she sipped her organic, GMO-free soy, decaffeinated, almond milk, Fair Trade cappuccino.

"A group of men sharing their deepest emotions, it'll be very healing..." she blinked at me like a hopeful, doe-eyed Bambi and something inside me died.

Bless her little hippie socks, she wants me to do emotions because she thinks it'll be good for me. So I, like a mug, was going to a healing workshop for men. Losing three hours of my life that could be spent shooting 3D bad guys on PlayStation with a flamethrower. I had visions of men sitting around in their underpants sobbing about being misunderstood, man-hugging, drum-beating, and blokes calling me 'bruvver'. Kill me.

I'd rather spend three days in the rat-infested trenches with enemy fire whistling past my ears than three hours in a 'safe circle' of men talking about my feelings.

Dread shadowed me until the night arrived where I sat in a circle with eight other men. The facilitator was Neil, aged 68. His first revelation was that - wait for it, this is big stuff - "women," he said, pausing for effect, "are driven by emotions and their hearts while men are ruled by logic and their heads." I glanced around the group. Nope, no one fell off their chair at this astounding insight.

Next, he said that women get frustrated when men don't listen to them. Ah yes, guilty. That one's me. I've mastered the art of moving my eyebrows and staring at the Tree Hugger so she thinks I'm listening to her when really I'm playing Call of Duty 3 in my head. When she catches me out, she is mad. Must get better at pretend listening. Perhaps introduce 'uhuh' and 'mmm' noises?

I glance at my watch. Ninety minutes in and not a single dirty joke. But then one of my fellow men's support groupers (MSGs) said he had a question about 'bedroom issues'. At last! We all leant forward, breaths held waiting for MSG to elaborate.

"How do you tell her that you hate what she's doing in the bedroom?" he asked, looking at each of us. Poor bloke. That chat would end in tears, no mistake.

"I agreed with her that we needed to spice things up in the bedroom but I didn't think that meant pink sheets and cushions..." Wait, hold on. He's talking about cushions? And that's when I did start crying. Neil passed me the tissues and whispered, "there there, that's right, let it all out, you're safe here..." while I sobbed into his shoulder. Tree Hugger was delighted when I told her. She said my emotional maturity was growing. At least I think that's what she said; I was moving my eyebrows about and shooting aliens with a flamethrower at the time.

CHAPTER THREE

BIKRAM YOGA FOR HARDCORE BLOKES

Yoga. That's all a bit pink and fluffy isn't it? When the Tree Hugger first suggested we do a yoga class, I internally snorted, figuring it would be about as tough as eating candy floss. After all, I spent 20 plus years running up hills in army boots at 5am with a backpack full of bricks and assault rifle over my shoulders. Yoga schmoga. However, it was a great chance to impress Tree Hugger with my stamina and virile manliness without even breaking a sweat.

"It's Bikram," she said, "you'll love it – it's brutal." Yoga? Brutal? Ha! Don't make me laugh. I Googled it. Sure enough, Bikram involves 26 postures, half of which you do lying down! Maybe I'd take that new Jeffrey Archer novel into class.

As it was my first time, the lady at the studio talked me through the rules. Happy days, I love rules and regimen.

"No talking, no drinking water unless the instructor tells you to, and no leaving the room during class," she barked. 'Good' I thought, 'stop any wimps from skiving.' Then off we went to put our mats and towels down in the hot room. 'A bit toasty,' I thought, 'it'll be like sunbathing'.

Class began with a weird breathing exercise while moving our elbows up and down followed by some arm twisting while sitting in a chair positions but there was no chair. Bah, child's play.

A balancing bit came next. Hmm. When did standing on one leg get so hard? Funny how what was easy at age seven isn't so easy 40 years later. What was wrong with me? I was shaking, straining, breathing hard and sweat was running off me in rivers; forming a pool around my feet. I glanced in the mirror; someone had replaced my head with a big, wet beetroot.

How much longer? Aghk! An hour? Another hour in this blistering torture chamber? Heaven have mercy. Oh thank goodness, we're lying down. Lucky, or I'd be falling down.

What? The lying down stuff is just as hard. During one pose, I almost cry out with pain. Oh no, I think I'm going to be sick, some pose named after a camel of all things is making me nauseous.

Normally, I think I've wasted my time unless I've exercised till I throw up but during yoga?! Finally, it was over. I could have filled a bath with the sweat wrung SEP out of my clothes. At least the sweat hid my tears of pain and relief. I hadn't felt SEP this bad since the 1988 Marines vs Special Forces in the 'last one dead wins' 36 hour extreme challenge. What madman came up with this accursed scorching torment? SEP I want to shake his hand! At last I'd found something that completely wrecked me. I was over the moon. This was my kind of workout - nausea-inducing. I love Bikram. I won't be telling Tree Hugger she was right though, not this side of hell freezing over - admitting that would be true torture.

CHAPTER FOUR

STUCK DEAD PEOPLE AND TALKING ROCKS

The Tree Hugger and I have been together a couple of years now so by now I've met all her friends. She kept me away from the weirdest ones for a while but now I know the truth.

Some of her friends see dead people. If the dead people are stuck, her friends try and get them to go through a tunnel. I can't see the tunnel. I can't see the dead people either. Apparently we had one of these stuck dead people in our villa. It kept switching our lights on and off. At least that's what Tree Hugger said, I wanted to get the electrician in but Tree Hugger's friends came round to persuade the stuck dead person to "walk towards the light".

I thought they were all batty at first but they're nice enough once you get to know them. Another thing her and her friends go on about is rocks. They call them crystals but they look like rocks to me. We have some huge rocks around the house, Tree Hugger says they do things like get rid of negative energy and fill your heart with love.

Back in my army days, we had to lift backpacks full of rocks over our heads and run around an obstacle course. Those rocks didn't seem to get rid of my negative energy. Nor did the pack of angry, snarling soldiers I was running alongside seem to have hearts filled with love. No point telling Tree Hugger that. She loves her rocks, she wears them as necklaces, rings, and ear-rings and has little bowls filled with polished coloured ones positioned all over the house.

"They have special powers," says Tree Hugger.

"Can they get me a cup of tea and a biscuit?" I ask. Tree Hugger didn't think that was as funny as I did.

One particular friend of hers, Sylvia, has rocks all over her house; she even takes them to bed with her. Goodness knows how her husband copes. She talks to them of course – all Tree Hugger's friends talk [SEP] to rocks and plants – the difference with Sylvia is that her rocks talk back to her and quite the conversation ensues.

Sylvia says that some of them have little spirits living inside them. I know this girl quite well [SEP] now and apart from hearing voices talking to her from rocks, she's a normal woman who's climbed high up the corporate ladder. She's even met Hillary Clinton. I wonder if Hillary talks to rocks. I guess some might argue that Bill could fit into that category. Not me though. I've always liked Bill. It seems ok to admit that again now.

Last week I said, "Show me one of your talking rocks Sylvia."

She brought out a clear crystal quartz about the size of her hand. "See, look inside," she said, "Can you see the little fairy?"

I peered inside. No. I could not see the little fairy.

"Say hello to her," said Sylvia.

"Hello fairy," I said to the rock. "Are you alright in there? It's not too cramped?" If my old Sergeant Major from Harrowgate could've seen me, he'd think I was stoned. And then he'd punch me.

CHAPTER FIVE

HOW TO SAVE THE WORLD BEFORE TEA TIME

The other night the Tree Hugger was sat with me and she asked one of those leftfield, curve ball questions. 'Babe, how do we make the world better?'

Yes, she was serious. Why was she asking me? Surely Obama and the Dalai Lama have that covered. Let's put this in perspective. That day, we'd been at a posh day spa where we'd both had a 90 minute massage followed by lots of strenuous laying by the pool alternating between slipping into the silky waters to cool off and reading a book (me, a critique of British manouvres in the Second World War; her, something about the Law of Attraction, a beauty book I assume).

That evening we'd dined at one of those restaurants where the chefs have their own TV shows and now we were settling in at our local pub. I had a large yeast-based beverage in one hand and had strategically positioned myself so that should the conversation get too 'new age' I could watch the footy being shown just over the Tree Hugger's left shoulder whilst grunting at intervals. For me, life couldn't get any better. Not unless Bernie Ecclestone came over and said, 'Neanderthal man, mate, I need you. Jenson's sick; can you take his place in the Formula One?"

Of course, Tree Hugger wasn't talking about the perfect little world we had created for ourselves that day. She was worried about melting polar caps, war orphans, child labour, oppression, poverty, racism, sexism, and bunnies being forced to wear lipstick. Anyway, there she sat, all earnest and sincere, with Man United scoring and the crowd going wild on top of her lovely head, "Babe, how do we make the world better?"

That's when 'bloke brain' kicked in and I said, 'Another bowl of potato wedges with sour cream would make it better.' Her expression made it clear that wasn't the right answer.

Truth is, I don't know. I love you Tree Hugger but I don't know! Buy Fair Trade coffee? Start a charity? Recycle your wine bottles? I don't know! Yes, [SEP]I get it; people are doing horrible things [SEP]to other people and animals all over the world but it's all too big and overwhelming. I need it breaking down into bite-sized chunks for my man-mind to cope. I wish I could make the world all unicorns and fluffy for you but I don't know how.

However, I have been thinking about it and what I've come up with is that I believe it starts with us all asking the question.

Ha! You didn't know I could be all deep did you!

If we keep asking ourselves, 'How we can leave our world better and kinder than when we left it?' maybe we'll all start coming up with our own answers.

Sorry, that's all I've got. Don't forget, I'm not called Neanderthal Man for nothing. If you want a book that'll help you save the world, go get something by Al Gore or Russell Brand.

Finally, Bernie, the answer is '[Gasp] OMG yes!' I can

start immediately and I'll be faster than Jenson, promise. Can I have a red car please? Maybe one with those flames down the side if it's not too much trouble?

CHAPTER SIX

HOSEPIPES AND BOTTOMS

The Tree Hugger recently decided that what I needed was a few colon hydrotherapy sessions.

"What's that when it's at home?" I asked. I shouldn't have because she told me. For the uninitiated, you basically get your insides washed out and it involves having a hosepipe up your backside with the tap turned on full. Just think 'reverse water boarding'. I'm sure it's illegal in some countries.

I've done a lot of these alternative and holistic treatments to keep the Tree Hugger happy and most of them I secretly enjoy, there's usually candles and lovely plinky plonky music involved, you just have to sit about and imagine you're in a forest or on the beach and no one shows any interest in hosepipes in relation to my bottom.

The last time any hands other[SEP] than my own had been 'down that [SEP] way' was in 1991 whilst I was serving as a soldier in Hong Kong. I was in hospital, seriously ill with heat stroke after an exercise on Lantau Peak during mid-summer, when a rather large male medic shoved a thermometer up my rear. I vowed that day to never again be defiled in such a way.

"It'll be good for you!" asserted Tree Hugger, who then went on to unnecessarily point out certain noxious symptoms of a less than sparkly digestive symptom. "I am a man, of course I have wind," I argued.

I was wasting my breath of course, as you men in long-term relationships out there will know. Once Tree Hugger had decided that a colon hydrotherapy treatment would be "really good" for me, it was a foregone conclusion that I'd soon find myself in a room with a nurse, a doctor's style examination table, a formidable looking machine with a whole pile of tubes.

After she weighed me and took my blood pressure, the nurse started to tell me what to expect. My fingers flew into my ears, 'LALALALALALALA...' I sang. I didn't want to know. Then she told me to take of ALL my clothes and put on a top that barely came down to my tummy button. So, there I was, 'tackle out' in front of a woman professionally trained in inserting tubes up rectums. 'Oh Tree Hugger,' I muttered, 'revenge will be mine...'

The nurse told me to lay on the table and passed me a rolled up towel, saying, "here, cuddle the teddy". Over the next hour, I cuddled that teddy like it's never been cuddled before. In some countries, I'd have to marry it after that level of intimacy. I don't like to be dramatic but it was the most traumatic experience of my life. I can't go into details, it's too distressing but I will carry the emotional scars for the rest of my days. This procedure should come with six months of post-stress counselling.

An hour in real time and three lifetimes in surreal time later, the ordeal was over and I was allowed to leave. Just before I hobbled home though, the nurse weighed me again. I was 600 grams lighter. That must be how much my dignity weighs. It was sucked away via that tube.

CHAPTER SEVEN

DETOXING IS FOR SISSIES

Detoxing. Whose bright idea was that then? The health evangelists would have me believe I'm loaded with toxins. Not sure I believe them. I've never seen any and don't know how they'd have gotten inside me. Do they hitchhike in on cheese toasties?

Tree Hugger though, has it in her lovely little head that we're full of these toxin things, whatever they are. She says this is very bad and that we need to get them out. How do you get them out? No surprises for guessing; it involves raw vegetables. Why can't toxins be flushed out with beer? Why can't they be chased away with ice-cream? It's just so typical. Raw flipping vegetables.

Yes, even I accept that we've been over indulging recently. The problem is, there's always a reason. Christmas, Valentine's, Easter, the sun's shining, the neighbour's cat had babies... and yes, perhaps blaming Tree Hugger for boil-washing my clothes till they shrunk was not an entirely accurate explanation for why I'm not fitting into my trousers so well anymore.

To do this detox, Tree Hugger booked us into a wellness resort for seven days. Apparently, we can't just eat vegetables at home. We need to pay an eye-watering fortune to have chefs highly trained in doing not very much with vegetables and seeds prepare our food. I can grate a carrot but you don't find me calling myself a gourmet wellness vegan chef.

Anyway, so we get to this resort and we're told that because we're on the detox diet, we can only have food from the buffet that has a yellow label. Any purple-labelled food is strictly off limits and all the staff had been briefed so don't try sneaking any, it would be confiscated. Naturally, there was to be no carbohydrates, caffeine or alcohol but we could have all the wheatgrass and spirulina juice we desired. No limits, knock ourselves out.

After the first day, I woke up with this strangely familiar gnawing feeling in my stomach. Then I remembered; it was hunger. Hadn't felt that in a while. We went up for breakfast. Not a sausage or piece of bacon in sight. Breakfast options were several vegetable dishes, vegetable soup, grapefruit, pumpkin seeds, salad (salad!) and all the herbal tea or caffeine-free coffee alternative sweetened with dried stevia leaves we could drink. Anything worth eating had a purple label and the breakfast buffet was guarded by a swarm of SS Waffen storm troopers dressed as waiters.

After breakfast, what were we going to do? The day stretched out in front of me like an infinite wail of internal pain. No TV! Entertainment options were: read a book; listen to a talk on nutrition; have some kind of therapy, and lay by the beach or pool. I read a lot of books that week. Cookbooks mostly, the pages are a bit sticky now from where my tears fell onto the recipes for mouth-watering delights like Beef Wellington ('... sit the beef fillet on a roasting tray, brush with olive oil...' sob...) and Chocolate Marquise ('... pour the melted chocolate into the butter mixture, and carefully stir...' boo hoo).

It was the longest week of my life. If this is detoxing, I'd rather keep my toxins thanks very much. I've told Tree Hugger that I'm choosing the next holiday, no arguments, I've earned it. There will be enough food and drink to sink a ship and an IMAX-sized, flat-screen TV in our room. But she really is going to have to stop boil washing my clothes.

CHAPTER EIGHT

HAPPY COWS AND CARNIVORES

Tree Hugger told me the other day that that she will no longer eat meat from "unhappy animals".

Up until now it's only been eggs. Tree Hugger refuses to buy eggs unless they've been laid by "happy chickens" that are free to roam in grassy fields. She feels strongly about the mental health of poultry. No surprises for guessing that the happy chicken eggs cost much more than the depressed chicken ones. I guess the extra money is needed for building chicken playgrounds and fun parks. Now it looks like the "happy animals" net is widening. Tree Hugger isn't opposed to eating meat in theory so we're not going vegetarian (thank the heavens and everything merciful); it's animal welfare that turns her into a 5ft 2" fire-spitting virago. Despite being a pacifist, hippie, throwback to the 60s, she'd happily take a machete to anyone who mistreats animals. So now, in the name of animal happiness, we have to figure out if our steak came from a contented cow and if we're eating fish fillets from cheerful tuna. It adds a whole new dimension of difficulty to a trip to the supermarket, which in my book is already one of the most hellish experiences on earth.

"How can you tell if it lived a happy life once it's dead?" I asked as we stared at the rows of shelves loaded with red meat. "How am I supposed to look at a bit of rib-eye steak or tray of mince meat and know if it came from a well-adjusted cow?" I continued. "And how

happy does it need to have been? Just kind of contented
with its lot or absolutely ecstatically happy?"

And how do you tell? I know they play classical music and
give massages to some of them cows in Japan for that
Wagyu beef, so I'm guessing those cows are happy but
frankly I can't afford to pay the extra for all that bovine
wellbeing therapy. Don't even mention MacDonalds to
Tree Hugger unless you want a lecture on the millions of
cows and chickens that live traumatic and miserable lives
then get killed each year to make cheap burgers and
nuggets. Systemised cruelty on a massive scale, according
to Tree Hugger. Apparently these animals are not happy
because they are confined with thousands of others in
cramped conditions and, as a result, they have to be
pumped full of all kinds of drugs to keep nasty diseases at
bay. Almost like animal nightclubbing.

Anyway, the upshot is that we're not buying any meat or
chicken unless it's free range. I hope that will keep Tree
Hugger happy but in truth, she'd like to see every animal
product come with a CV of the animal that died for it
printed on the pack. It's name (eg, Dolly the sheep) and
farm of origin, Dolly's general happiness grade, snapshots
of Dolly frolicking happy in lush grass, and assurances that
death was painless and unexpected. The farmer had crept
up from behind, said, 'look over there...' and it was all
over before Dolly had a chance to say, 'baaa byeee'.

CHAPTER NINE

GO ON, FEEL MY CHAKRAS

I'm pretty well versed at all this hippie stuff now. I even know about things like chakras. There are seven main ones dotted up your spine to the top of your head. I'm not sure what they do though.

Recently the Tree Hugger took me along to one of her whacky workshops. This one was about learning to feel someone else's chakras. 'Awesome,' I thought, when she told me, I knew I'd probably be the only bloke; I had an idea of where some of those chakras were and I had full consent from the Tree Hugger to feel other people's, the day was looking up.

So we get there and it started with all the usual full body embracing, air kissing, complimenting one another on how great their aura was looking, all while a CD of Om chanting to Tibetan singing bowls played in the background.

When the mutual aura appreciation was done, the workshop kicked off and as luck would have it, Tree Hugger was pulled up to be part of the first demo.

The lady who was teaching us about feeling chakras started patting the air around Tree Hugger, stopping about six inches from her body.

"There you are, can you see I am touching the edge of her chakra?" she asked the group. "Can you see how well developed her heart chakra is?" Everyone nodded seriously and murmured things like 'oh yes' and 'mmm definitely'. I looked as hard as I could but for the life of me I couldn't see Tree Hugger's heart chakra. But I joined in all the head nodding anyway and mumbled, 'yes, very big, just lovely...' and hoped they didn't guess I wasn't talking about her chakra.

Then it was our turn to practise on each other. If I do say so myself, I put on an Oscar-winning performance. Like I'd seen that French mime artist Marcel Marceau do when he was pretending to be stuck behind a wall, I moved my hands slowly around my partner's torso like I was feeling for something. After a bit of this, complete with furrowed brow to suggest deep, trance-like concentration, I pretended that I couldn't bring my hands any closer to my partner because I'd hit an invisible barrier. The teacher congratulated me but Tree Hugger shot me one of those warning looks that suggested she wasn't fooled.

In the car on the way home, I said to Tree Hugger, "So, um, did you, ah, could you... actually feel anything?" She sat suspiciously still for a moment and then said, "Well, I think so... I'm not sure..." We stared at the road ahead in contemplation. Had everyone in the group been pretending? Was it like The Emperor's New Chakras? That's when I saw the opportunity. So I'm holding my first life-transforming workshop next month. Come along, I'll teach you how to see auras and feel chakras for an energy exchange of just $5,000. Be quick! Limited spaces! Sign up at www.ChakraScam.ae.

CHAPTER 10

NAMASTE, GOING TO A PARTY

The other week, the Tree Hugger told me we'd be spending the coming Friday night at her friend's house party in Emirates Hills. I could barely contain my excitement. This house was amazing. More like a Hollywood mansion, it had a huge swimming pool and Jacuzzi, its own cinema, a barbeque with NASA technology for literally space-age sausages... images swum through my mind of midnight swimming and endless drinks with umbrellas in them, eating my body weight in burnt meat drowned in tomato sauce, uninhibited dancing to cheesy music and loud singing of what I thought were the lyrics. I could not wait. A chance to really let my hair down when someone else was paying was long overdue.

The next few days crept slowly. I passed the time with karaoke singing practise, "Wahhhh AHHHH! Livin' on a pray-ehh, take my hand, we'll make it I swear-ehh..."

Finally the evening arrived and that's when Tree Hugger said something deeply worrying: "I'll drive tonight if you want Babe..." 'Drive?' What's this 'drive' nonsense? Why on earth would we take the car? Surely we'll only have to abandon it and then collect it the next day with a banging head. Far more sensible to take a taxi, I said. Then she said, "You are going to behave yourself tonight, aren't you?" Again, a deeply worrying comment that I didn't feel I could truthfully answer until the word 'behave' was clearly defined. Alarm bells were going off in my head like a fleet of fire trucks at an arsonists' convention. 'Drive?' 'Behave?' What kind of party was this?

As we drove up, I could've seen the house from a mile away. It was emblazoned with lights and music was blaring. My heart fell. This was not Bon Jovi screeching about living on a prayer. This was new agey, plinky plonky music that really was a prayer.

The blood drained from my face as the full horror of my situation crystallised. I was spending my precious Friday night with Tree Hugger's wacky chakra-cleansing, moon-howling, almond-milk-with-organic-coffee drinking mates.

As we walked through the front door, I was accosted by a smiling blonde man called Colin. He dabbed a red dot between my eyebrows, put a string of flowers around my neck, and handed me a tambourine. Then he pressed his hands together in prayer, bowed his head and said, 'namaste'. Oh noooo... I wailed, biting on my tambourine. Not 'namaste', please Lord, no, not a 'namaste' party.

"Tree Hugger!" I snarled quietly once we'd stepped out of earshot of Colin, "What on earth is this about?" She blinked those big doe-like eyes at me. "I told you Babe, we're celebrating the equinox and using it to manifest abundance with meditation and mantras. Come on, let's grab a chai tea and a gluten-free samosa before the chanting begins, you're going to love this, I think it'll really move you..."

Her words cut into my heart like an icy knife. No umbrella drinks, no sausages cooked on the NASA barbeque, no falling into the swimming pool with all my clothes on... as always when faced with difficult life decisions, I asked myself, 'what would Jon Bon Jovi do?' [SEP] I had to face the truth. These days, Jon would probably pour a chai tea, text his mate Sting to come on over, sit cross-legged and settle in for a four-hour chanting marathon. I turned to Tree Hugger as tears ran down my cheeks.

"Aw Babe, I told you you'd find this really moving," she whispered. "Just close your eyes and feel the energy in your heart chakra…"

Oh yes, living on a bloody prayer.

CHAPTER 11

SAVING THE SLAVE CHICKENS

I've been worried about chickens lately. Worried to the point of obsession. It started when Tree Hugger made me watch one of them horrific videos on YouTube that show how the poor little mites are kept prisoners in tiny cages where they're so traumatised and miserable that all their feathers fall out.

Honestly, sometimes I wish she'd just let me live in blissful ignorance. Since watching that video, I've had nightmares about turning into a giant chicken and being forced to lay eggs all day in a cell so small I can't turn around. A couple of nights ago, I woke up screaming about omelettes and yesterday in Spinneys supermarket I burst into tears when a woman put a box of eggs laid by caged hens in her trolley. "No, please no," I pleaded through tears, "don't support this barbarism. Look, buy these free range eggs from this lovely organic farm in the Irish countryside… for the love of chickens, please lady, do it for the chickens…"

I think she went to get security but Tree Hugger hustled me out of there and into a café for a nice cup of tea and a sit down where she stroked my head and said 'there there' a lot while I told her about how we had to do something to save the chickens.

I have a friend in the UK who keeps chickens in his garden. He rescued the old girls from one of those awful battery farms that was going to kill them. Battery chickens tend to get destroyed after just a year of life – I say 'life' but it's more like 'living hell' - however their natural lifespan is about five years and they can lay eggs for most of that time.

I want some rescue chickens! I want to liberate some imprisoned hens from captivity and nurse them back from being featherless and traumatised to happy, healthy and feathery.

In the UK, rescuing battery hens has become quite a movement but not so in the UAE. I'm not sure how chickens would cope with being in the garden in Dubai's summer though. I guess we'll have to let them in the house when it's hot. I'm sure Tree Hugger will be ok with that. We can put them in the spare bedroom. Chickens make great pets; apparently they're really affectionate. And we'd have an endless supply of free-range eggs! So if our two cats object to the new family members, I'll point out that at least the chickens contribute to the household. That, frankly, the cats had been freeloading for too long and it was time to get their paws dirty. But maybe the cats will come to love the chickens like feathered sisters and then we'll film them all doing something cute and funny, it'll go viral on YouTube and make us millions. Yeah, that'd be eggcellent.

CHAPTER 12

HANDS UP! I'M A HEALER

In my former life, pre-Tree Hugger, when I wasn't feeling well, I would call in sick at work and head off to see my local doctor.

Old Dr Ridley would take my blood pressure, peer down my throat with something that looking like a wooden stick from an ice lolly, get me to stand on the weighing scales and then invariably tell me to take a couple of days off work and watch telly from the sofa with a hot water bottle and lots of fluids. Sometimes he gives me antibiotics to take depending on whether it's just a cold or the obviously far more life-threatening and very serious man-flu.

Tree Hugger, on the hand, doesn't go to doctors very often. She goes to healers. And she goes to them a lot. In fact, in the years I've known her she's been to the doctor maybe once but in that time she must've had about 60 sessions with people who call themselves a 'healer'.

The word 'healer' seems to encompass a wide and varied array of talents and abilities as well. Some of whom charge an eye-watering amount of money for what they do – which can sometimes be as little as wave their hands around Tree Hugger for 30 minutes or so. Not even touching her! This can be called anything from Reiki to hands-on healing, pranic healing… and if they wave their hands around while holding a rock, they call it crystal therapy and then it becomes even more expensive. For the amount of money that Tree Hugger's spent on having people wave crystals at her, I could've bought a new motorbike. But no, she's the one getting taken for a ride.

Tree Hugger doesn't care thought, she loves all this stuff. Even when she comes home from a session and doesn't really know what the healer did. She'll say something like, 'ah, well, they had to remove some negative psychic attack energy from my auric field and clear some old emotional stuff from my heart chakra…'

Let's assume for a minute that the healer really did those things. What does it achieve? Nothing that's obvious to me. Tree Hugger was fine and healthy when she went to see them and she is fine and healthy when she comes back. They don't even give her a nice cream to rub on.

"You don't understand," Tree Hugger will say. "Toxic old emotions and trauma will manifest into physical ailments if you don't get it all cleared out of your energy field…"

On many occasions she has tried to explain to me in more detail about the connection between our energy bodies and physical bodies but I get lost in a cloud of incomprehensible new age hippie speak. Words like 'vibration', 'negative entities', 'manifest' and Sanskrit names for chakras like Mooladhara… I'd only just gotten my head around the idea of having a root chakra when she then goes and starts calling it by its Sanskrit name.

The problem for me is that you can't actually see any of these energy bodies. If one of these healers could show me my root chakra like a doctor can show me my ribcage on x-ray then I might be able to get more on board with this whole energy bodies thing. But you have to take it on trust.

"Oh dear," some healer will say. "Your heart chakra is clogged with unprocessed pain from childhood but don't worry, I'll clear that out now by channeling healing frequencies through the palms of my hands… your angels are helping with this…"

And you just have to believe them! I can't see anything coming out of her hands; I can't see my angels, and I can't feel anything happening. But I can see the money from my wallet going into her till afterwards. I feel it too. Oh yes, that's all very real.

So yes, when one of Tree Hugger's friends calls themself a 'healer' (and every single one of them does), part of me sniggers and another part of me takes tighter hold of my wallet. You can imagine my delight then when Tree Hugger announced she'd booked me on a weekend workshop to learn a new thing called ThetaHealing. She wanted me to be able to call myself a 'healer'.

Tree Hugger and all her mates are raving about ThetaHealing. It's their Fave New Thing. They huddle together in vegan cafes wearing cruelty-free organic lipstick and drinking turmeric oat milk lattes, talking about how it's on the cutting edge of spiritual healing… I just quietly read my latest issue of Motorcycle News when they start with all that but despite my best efforts, I still manage to hear a lot of their conversation. So when Tree Hugger tells me the 'good news' about spending a weekend to learn this healing technique, I already have an idea that the 'theta' part of its name is taken from a brainwave cycle and I have to admit (though never, ever to Tree Hugger and her friends) that this part is actually interesting. You see, in the army, I trained in telecommunications engineering so I know that theta is a frequency range of four to seven cycles per second, or Hertz. And as a telecommunications engineer anything with a frequency, no matter how low, can't be all bad.

The theta frequency range is the brainwave that we go into when we're on the edge of sleep. This isn't just hippie talk, this has been measured numerous times and so is scientifically proven. That's right! Scientifically proven! Something that Tree Hugger is involved with actually has something in it that's scientifically proven and not just 'proven' by dowsing it with a pendulum.

To me and my esteemed colleagues in the field of telecommunications, it is extremely unjust, nay, frankly criminal, that your average person doesn't understand or recognise the hugely important role that frequency plays in our modern lives.

Now, I don't want to bore you but let's not forget that everything we hold dear relies on frequencies. From radio, to television, microwave ovens, Bluetooth, and of course our beloved mobile phones. So, I was at least partly hopeful that, if nothing else, I could talk long and hard to my fellow healing course participants about the beauty of frequencies. Plus of course, there was the small matter of earning brownie points with Tree Hugger to last till the Christmas after next.

So, I dutifully turned up on that first morning and quickly discovered I would be the only bloke on the course. No surprise there. All the real blokes were doing proper man stuff like riding their bikes, kicking or throwing some kind of ball, making important things with wood or metal, or lain prostate on the sofa with a six pack of lager, the remote control and 12 hours of car racing on Sky Sport.

Me? No. I was stuck in a room for two days with a bunch of crystal-wearing women who knew the names of their spirit guides.

So, as is my approach to all of the things Tree Hugger gets me to do, I resigned myself to my fate and waited to see what type of madness would unfold this time.

Things began in territory with which I was comfortable, namely, discussion of the theta frequency range. Hurray! Science stuff! Well, close enough.

Theta is the brainwave frequency range that hypnotherapists aim to put their patients in so that they can delve deeply into their subconscious minds. ThetaHealing works the other way round though. It's the healer – as opposed to the healee – who puts themselves into the theta brainwave state and then 'connects' to the client's energy. And this is where things quickly spiral off back into new age hippie land because the route you are supposed to take in order to 'connect' to your client's energy is via a visit to the edge of the universe where God lives.

Yes, you read that right. It was all going so well with all the talk of scientifically proven brainwave frequencies but then the hippies have to throw God into the mix. Although in ThetaHealing, they don't like to use the word God so much because apparently it's too much of a misunderstood and loaded term so they prefer to say the 'Creator Of All That Is'.

They say we're referring to an intelligent consciousness

and you can call it whatever you like – Higher Intelligence, Source, The Divine, Allah, The Universe, Spirit… which to my mind sounds like they don't really know what it is and are hedging their bets but I decide it's best to not argue the toss about that just now. We're only 40 minutes into the workshop and have a whole day, seven hours and 23 minutes still left to get through. Best not poke the hippie bears in the chakras too much just yet.

I get 'energy' though. Again, that's scientifically proven. Plus, I don't think there's a married man alive who doesn't understand the concept of sensing energy. You know without any shadow of a doubt when your wife's energy field is black in colour and is coming at you like a thousand razor blades. I don't care how often she insists through gritted teeth that, "nothing's wrong, I'm FINE!"

So yes, us humans are full of energy or electricity so I can also get my head around the notion of people's energy fields touching or overlapping with other peoples.

When you're in a crowded room, you know someone is staring at you because you suddenly have the urge to turn around and you catch their eye, that is energy. So yeah, I'm on board with that it's just when the hippies have to add in things like angels and talking to dead people that I think, 'well, you just ruined it…'

Also when the ThetaHealing teacher says that we can connect to someone else's energy and then heal them with the power of our minds, well, again that's just one little hippie step too far but for now I'll play along.

So on that first morning, the teacher taught us how to get

ourselves into the theta brainwave state and connect to Creator through a meditation that involves imagining ourselves sitting in a golden ball hovering just above our heads, then travelling upwards in this ball through space and past galaxies, through some jelly stuff, past pink clouds and into a huge ball of pearly white light.

So far so tolerable but the worst was yet to come, namely my most dreaded and loathed activity at group workshops. We were told to pair up and practice on one another. Aggghk! Partner work!

So there I was, sitting opposite an Arab lady whilst trying to, ahem, connect to her energy. The idea was that we would mentally scan our partner's physical and emotional bodies and see if we could get any information that could 'prove' we were connecting to them, eg, 'I can see you've broken your right arm at some point' or 'I can see you're the eldest of three sisters and have three children yourself...'

So I sat and concentrated on the lady in front of me trying to 'see' inside her. Minutes grind slowly by but I'm getting nothing.

Nothing, zip, not a sausage, there was no connection for me or magic message to tell me that the lady I was trying to scan enjoyed baking cup cakes, had 26 siblings or was one of the long lost survivors of the titanic.

Thankfully, that exercise was called to a finish and it was time for more theory learning. My mind wandered to how much fun I would be having had I gone on the bike ride that all my mates had gone on. I was feeling fairly sorry for myself, not only was I wasting my time there and missing what would no doubt be a great ride I also knew the ridicule I'd have to endure from my mates should they ever find out my reason for not going on the ride with them. Their wives weren't hippies. Their wives did things like play tennis and take pottery classes not talk to dead people and cleanse crystals at midnight on a full moon.

Soon it was time for another practice with a partner. This time we had to scan a new partner to see if we could find any genetic defect in their family line, and which side of the family line it had come from, that could make them ill in the future.

'No problem,' I thought. 'I'll just say she has diabetes in the family'. Just about every Arab family in Dubai has diabetes these days so I'll just say that and then we can break for coffee.

So there I was, sat in a Muslim country holding hands with a veiled Arabic lady. It was probably a crime just touching her hand let alone holding her hands. Then it happened. The word 'breasts' pinged into my head. 'Stop it! I hissed at myself in my mind. 'I am not saying anything about this lady's breasts, we are going to talk about diabetes!'

Mentioning this woman's breasts to her would probably get me thrown into a Dubai gaol, I argued to whoever was inside my head telling me to tell her about her breasts. But no, this voice was adamant, insistent even, that I needed to tell this woman about a problem with her breasts.

So, I just gave her the information that the pushy bloke inside my head was providing. I told her that I thought she may have a problem with her breasts and that it had come from her mother's side of the family.

The Arabic lady said nothing.

I stammered on regardless. I told her that I was able to see two dark lumps on her breasts and that I was able through the technique we had just been taught, to make these go away, so I did. I made the command to Creator and then watched as I imagined the two dark lumps floating up and away.

To my massive relief, the session was then over and I escaped as fast as I could to the coffee area. Perhaps this is where the police would arrest me once that lady had made the call. As I poured milk into my cup, she walked over to me. From the corner of my eye, I could see the fabric of her black abaya swishing with each step.

She came to stand beside me and asked if we could talk. I held my breath waiting for words like 'charlatan' and 'inexcusable' but she went on to explain that her Aunt, her mother's sister, had just died of breast cancer and her mother was recovering from it. She said breast cancer was prevalent in her mother's side of the family with almost all women suffering from it during their lives.

I was bowled over. Where had that voice in my head come from? How did it know about her family history? You're not telling me that this ThetaHealing stuff is actually a thing? Something that actually works? But how can that be? It's not science!

Since that workshop, I've done a little more training and had a few sessions with other people. I don't get a strong connection with everybody but I can sometimes get a great connection and when I do, that voice in my head tells me some incredible and accurate stuff about them. It's like this fun game that I didn't know existed. No, I can't explain it to you. Maybe the scientists will be able to explain it one day – something about DNA information transfer when energy fields overlap or information transmission via brainwave frequency. Maybe in one hundred years, it'll be as normal to people then as it is for us to talk to someone on the other side of the planet through a small glass and metal box we hold in our hand. Heck, I don't know. All I know is that I better not start seeing dead people or that will require a long and awkward visit to Dr Ridley.

CHAPTER 13

AYAHUASCA THE SPIRITUAL BARK SMOOTHIE

It took her about three years of gentle cajoling but just like the bubbling yet persistent stream that slowly erodes the granite rock, Tree Hugger finally got me to agree to spending a week in a forest with a bunch of strangers to drink some potion made from Amazonian plants so I could talk to God.

Yep, a plant drink that gets you talking to God. And I mean properly, actually talk to God with God talking back and us having quite the in-depth conversation. Not the usual type of talking to God where it's all me doing the talking and pleading and God not really seeming to do much in the way of listening or replying.

This Amazon forest drink is called ayahuasca and I really didn't want to do it. In my whole life, I have never taken any drugs other than alcohol that you can't buy in your local pharmacy. And let's not forget, ayahuasca is illegal everywhere in the world except places like Peru. There might be a really good reason for that. What's more it's probably only legal in Peru because the country would economically crumble if the endless stream of western hippies arriving to drink psychedelics under the pretext of having a spiritual awakening suddenly dried up.

The Peruvian officials probably sit round drinking coffee in meeting rooms saying '*yes, well of course it's the most stupid thing in the world but these rich westerners seem to like it so let's just cash in before the rest of the world realises what they're missing out on and starts legalising it as well… and why fight it? Look at the mess those Americans have created with their useless so-called war on drugs. Just say no my bottom… now, pass me those biscuits would you please Juan?'*

Me and Tree Hugger weren't going to Peru though. We were headed to a log cabin in a forest in a remote part of Holland thanks to the liberal Dutch attitudes to this kind of thing. Now, the Dutch authorities don't officially say taking ayahuasca is legal but when asked they kind of shuffle their feet, mumble about not really recommending that sort of thing but then basically turning a blind eye.

If you're wondering how to pronounce 'ayahuasca', it's basically 'eye-ah-wass-ka', which is also the sound you yell into your plastic bucket after drinking it but more on that later.

Ayahuasca is a thick greenish beverage brewed with two plants that grow in the Amazon jungle. They call it a 'tea' but it's like no cup of tea that my mum ever made. It's a bit like drinking a thick smoothie made of bark and leaves, but worse.

The bit that gets everyone so excited and outraged is the DMT that the brew contains. DMT is a proper psychedelic drug. Its official sciencey name is dimethyltryptamine but its nickname is 'the spirit molecule' and traditionally, it's used by the indigenous people of the Peruvian Amazon region for spiritual and healing purposes.

DMT is actually a naturally occurring substance in many plants and animals, including humans, but normally when we consume it, our stomachs have some kind of enzyme that destroys the DMT so we don't get high as kites. This is where the clever plants of the Amazon come in because one of the two plants in the brew deactivates this process and allows the DMT to do its stuff unhindered.

Of course, loads of Tree Hugger's friends have done ayahuasca and we've spent many hours listening to their wild descriptions of the other worlds and fantastical creatures they met during their trips.

And naturally, they say, these experiences were profound and life changing. Tree Hugger's mates talked about their chakras blowing wide open, achieving enlightenment, chatting with their spirit guides and finally knowing what it was to feel profound connection to everything in the universe. One of her friends says she understood the meaning and purpose of human life itself from God's perspective during one session. Unfortunately, she just couldn't remember what it was when the ayahuasca wore off.

Tree Hugger couldn't get enough of these stories. She so desperately wanted to drink this magic potion and have a doorway to another dimension open up in front of her so she could go off and talk to some archangel who starred in the Bible or an alien being from the Pleidian star system.

Truth be told, it wasn't all unicorns and cherubs though. Our friends also reported that a great deal of 'purging' took place. This is a nicer way of saying uncontrollable vomiting and diarrhoea. Then there was the abject terror, paranoia, and being faced with their worst fears bit. One of our friends who had a snake phobia found herself being swallowed by a gigantic black mamba in her ayahuasca hallucination and yes, she was terrified at the time. Another friend had what they call in ayahuasca circles 'a little death'. He genuinely thought something had gone wrong and he was actually dying. He tried writing a goodbye note to his wife and kids but found he couldn't hold a pen.

Trouble is, Tree Hugger only focuses on the nice stories about angels and enlightenment while I can't get past the phobia, paranoia and purging.

I fought the inevitable for as long as I could but it was only a matter of time. So off we were to spend precious annual leave holiday time in a Dutch forest with hippie strangers drinking bark smoothies while clinging onto plastic buckets.

Naturally, when you embark on one of these life quests you want to know you're in safe and reliable hands. So we trawled the internet and picked someone who had a nice website. We filled in the online questionnaire and waited to see whether we would be accepted – they don't take just anyone you know.

"Hurray!" squealed the excited Tree Hugger, clapping her little hands in delight when we got the email a few days later confirming we'd been found acceptable enough to pay them a huge amount of money for providing us with bark smoothies and plastic buckets in a cramped log cabin. 'Hurray…' I echoed, my voice trailing away.

Then came the list of pre-retreat instructions. For at least a month before the week-long retreat, we were to stop having alcohol, caffeine, dairy, pork and beef. We were also supposed to have no sex. Suddenly I was at least looking forward to the retreat so that it could all be over quicker.

The long-awaited day finally came and after a flight to Holland we were greeted at the airport by a man who introduced himself as Brother as well as a very nice young Dutch guy who I will call Left Hand Man, or Lefty, as he always sat to Brother's left hand side during the ayahuasca ceremonies. There were seven of us doing the retreat, three women and four men.

Brother and Lefty shoehorned our merry group into two small cars. The boot space in the car was enough to fit a matchbox so we stacked our bags on our knees till they touched the roof and settled in for a half hour drive through the Dutch countryside.

As we rumbled over the pristine Dutch roads, the suspension in our valiant little vehicle creaked and groaned beneath the weight of adults and enough luggage to support Madonna on her next world tour.

"Did you not tick the 'luxury' box on the website?" I whispered to Tree Hugger. "When do we get offered bottles of chilled Evian water and rolled up lavender scented washcloths?" She scowled at me and hissed a 'shush'.

A while later we were at our destination which was a small log cabin in the middle of a wood far away from civilisation. Well, a good couple of miles anyway. Our neighbours were large Dutch dairy cows.

The setting was beautiful, a little cold at that time of year, and quiet with just the noise of birds singing and the breeze rustling through the trees. There were walking paths all around the forest and this seemed like the ideal place to hold a spiritual retreat. The little cabin had two communal bedrooms and a main room with a kitchen dining area and a sitting area at the other end. The toilets, shower and washbasins were in another building outside. The shower had hot water but the basins were strictly cold water only so it would be cold washes in the morning as well as a cold walk with a torch at night if you needed the loo.

We met the final member of the hosting party trio in the cabin. She was a young Dutch lady who was the partner of Left Hand Man. She always sat on Brother's right hand side during the ceremonies. Right Hand Lady and Left Hand Man were there to help Brother with the ceremonies as well as to look after all of us by feeding us, guiding us through the daily routine and helping us with whatever we needed. While Brother went to his house in a nearby village every evening, Righty and Lefty spend the whole week with us sleeping and eating in the cabin.

Me and Tree Hugger shared a room with the three other males on the retreat. It was a bunk bed situation and there was barely enough room for two people to stand up at the same time.

"Did you not tick the box for a king-size bed with ensuite bathroom on the website?" I asked Tree Hugger. Apparently not. She must've accidentally ticked the 'damp sleeping bag on child-sized bunk bed with outside bucket and torch' box.

In truth, I felt quite comfortable in this sparse, basic environment where information about the week's programme seemed to be on a 'need to know' basis. I have been on countless courses in the Army where information is withheld to see how we cope. Limiting preparation time keeps people on their toes, you see.

Another throw back to my military days was that each morning we were to stand outside in our swimsuits and pour three buckets of icy cold water over our heads before then leaping into a Swedish-style, log-burning, open-air hot tub.

The Tree Hugger struggled with the icy water but cold showers were nothing new to me. I felt that throwing the hot tub in was a bit of a namby pamby cop out. So far I was happily slipping into a military-style resilience - remote location, limited information and cold showers, right up my street.

That first evening there was to be no ayahuasca ceremony. Instead we were going to get to know each other better. We were to sit around a campfire and introduce ourselves. Oh God. I dread this kind of touch feely stuff, it's my absolute worst nightmare. I wondered if they'd already slipped some ayahuasca to us in the herbal tea and I was going through a little death of facing my deepest fears. I must've been on some kind of psychedelic though because, when it came to my turn to tell the group what I was hoping to gain from the week ahead, I heard myself saying that I was there to open my connection to spirit in the hope that it would guide me on the path to spiritual awakening.

Holy Mary Mother of God where on earth did that come

from? I turned to look at Tree Hugger but she was just beaming back at me in a proud kind of way and I felt vaguely sick. Whatever she was doing was working. I was turning into a thoroughbred hippie tree hugger myself. Note to self, check that stuff she's been sprinkling on my granola. And start weight-lifting.

The first ayahuasca ceremony was held on the second evening after a day of DIY cold water buckets, outdoor yoga, tiny portions of bland vegetarian food, and more touch feely self exploration.

I could feel the testosterone draining from me by the hour. Finally, the clock rolled around to ayahuasa time and we all prepared for the first encounter with Mother Ayahuasca, who is said to be the divine feminine spirit that lives within the plant. I pulled on a pair of grayish white cotton trousers and a was-once-white t-shirt as we'd been asked to wear white clothing for the ceremonies. Yes, these experiences are conducted over about five hours or so with all the ritual, pomp and ceremony of a sacred or religious event.

Everyone picked a spot on the sofas placed in a semi-circle around a log fire and settled in for a long night. Ominously, each spot had blankets, a toilet roll, torch, and a bucket for mouth-related purging. We were told to ask Righty or Lefty for help getting to the outside toilet if we needed bottom-related purging. I prayed to any god that was listening to please, please not let me need to ask for help getting to the outdoor loo.

And so the ceremony began. Brother was sat cross-legged on the floor at the head of our semi-circle in front of a makeshift altar featuring eagle feathers, crystals and rocks, various exotic looking pipes, candles, burning sage, and other ornamental bits and pieces as well as two large plastic bottles of a dark, green liquid. This was the ayahuasca brew itself. We gazed at it in silent reverence. I wondered why they'd used such cheap bottles for the holy beverage but decided not to ask. Anyway, things were beginning.

First up, Brother offered each one of us a type of snuff powder called rapé. Using a very long-stemmed bamboo tube contraption. Brother basically blows this stuff up your nostril. There seems to be a lot of spitting and wretching involved as he does this. One of the girls tried the rapé first and basically started throwing up immediately so I decided to pass on the sacred snuff, despite the promise that it would help clear our minds to make way for the ayahuasca and enhance our experience. No, I'm good, thanks anyway.

At last it was time to drink and this is where the ceremony bit really kicked in. The theme was native American Indian meets new age hippie on Ecstacy with a sprinkling of Peruvian shaman.

Going round the circle one by one, Brother gestured to each of us in turn to join him at the altar. The idea was that you sat opposite Brother, he chanted something tribal and fanned sage smoke at you with his feathers then with both hands he ceremoniously handed you a cup of ayahuasca and bowed his head. You received the cup with a bow, then held it up as you turned and acknowledged each of the people in the circle one by one, you then hold the cup to your heart and silently tell Mother Aya what you want to experience, then you say 'Kau-Say-Pah' out loud and down the drink in one go. If you can. You then work very hard to not immediately throw it back up. The stuff is fairly vile and it takes some effort to hold it down.

So, I stumbled my way through all that with no major incident and returned to my spot on the sofa. The nervous waiting began. There was no going back now. The divine Mother had me by the proverbials. However, looking around the group, it was some small comfort to see that none of the people who had drank before me were doing anything strange. Yet.

So I sipped on my bottle of water and waited. My ears throbbed with the loud drumming music that Brother had playing on the stereo as we all sat not speaking while waiting anxiously to see who would be first to get sucked into another dimension of craziness.

My first realisation that something was amiss was the sensation of pins and needles that started spreading through my body. 'Here we go,' I thought, taking a deep breath. Next, the skin of my face transformed into plasticine and apparently some invisible sculptor was manipulating it into strange shapes. The sensation then changed into one that I was more familiar with, that of extreme nausea caused – usually - by drinking far too much alcohol.

Unsure about which end of me would explode first, I made a prompt exit and headed to the outdoor loo. I say 'prompt exit' but in fact what I did was stagger like a new born foal towards the door as my legs did not seem to belong to me anymore. I also clinged to my bucket like a drowning man clings to a lifebuoy and am not proud to say that I did not make it to the loo.

Happily though, it was the mouth-purging that kicked in first and the bucket rose admirably to the challenge. I then continued on my quest to reach the toilet under the impression that the purging was unfinished. My sense of relief on arriving at my destination was, I imagined, what Edmund Hillary and Tenzing Norgay must have felt on reaching the summit of Everest.

Once there, I didn't move from the hallowed throne for a very long time whilst still regularly calling out for my best friend Huey in the bottom of the bucket. My t-shirt was dripping with sweat and again it felt a lot like the aftermath of one of those 24-hour non-stop binge drinking sessions we would do back in my much younger, squaddie days.

Eventually though, some decision was made by some part of me to rejoin the group. I staggered the 20 metres or so back to the cabin and as I walked in the door, preparing to navigate my way back to my position on the sofa, the hallucinatory scene in front of me was that everyone else in the group was sitting on the floor doing the Gap Bands "oops upside your head" dance from the 1970s. For those unfamiliar with this dance, it's kind of like a seated conga line.

I was convinced that was what I was seeing but a few minutes later, my vision reshaped the scene and I realised they were doing nothing of the sort. In fact, everyone was still sat in their allotted places on the sofa, caught up in their own internal drama as loud drumming music and singing played in the background.

I settled in from that point to see what would happen, using the philosophy that I had now done this so I may as well embrace it and go with the flow. The uncontrollable plasticine face manoeuvres kicked in again and then things started to get really quite deep, I have to admit. It was like having a conversation with someone inside my head who was much wiser than me. Was this God?

I was asking myself all sorts of difficult questions and getting answers that normally would never come. Really clever and insightful answers. This Voice was basically telling me to take control of my own life. The Voice told me to stop drinking alcohol, and to stop being so focused on earthly time as it was just an illusion. It also told me that, although tonight's ayahuasca experience was a positive thing for me to do, I would gain no benefit from doing any more and in fact it would be better if I did not drink the brew again in future. Then my mum popped into my head for a chat. I should mention that my mum has been dead about 30 years and I know that many people reading this might think I was just hallucinating, and maybe I was but at the time, I promise you, it was very convincing. I was sure I was talking to my mum. Plus she brought with her a couple of other ancestors for a chat too, like my grandfather, which was nice.

I took the opportunity to apologise to her for having been a bit of a swine as a kid and she said not to worry about that, I'd been a child and it was part of growing up. She said she was happily 'living' on the other side with the rest of our family who had passed over.

Another thing that was definitely worthy of note was the incredible sense of hearing I had during the whole experience. It felt like the music emanated from within me, as if me and the music were one and the same, much more so than even wearing the world's best set of headphones.

After a few hours, the effects started to wear off, ending as it had begun with that pins and needles sensation. The ayahuasca world I visited dissolved and my usual view of reality swam back into place. I spent the last hour watching what was going on with the rest of the group. During the ceremony, we had all been offered top ups of the ayahuasca to drink. Some people took more but I declined. The lights went up at about 3am and there was tea and fruit for whoever wanted it but me and Tree Hugger went straight to bed.

The following day, the group debriefed in the hot tub after the three self-inflicted cold water buckets. Everybody had had differing amounts of purging and different types of experience. A couple of people had positive experiences like mine, one person had a neutral experience where not much happened, which she was disappointed about and everyone else had harrowing, difficult or upsetting experiences, although they felt 'lighter' as a result, they said. That whole thing about coming face to face with your demons and emerging out the other side. From some of the descriptions though, those demons can be quite the challenge, the biggest and toughest men in our group had been reduced to uncontrollable floods of tears.

We were supposed to do two more ceremonies after that first one but after being advised by The Voice that it'd be better if I didn't drink any more ayahuasca, I told Brother I would be standing down for the next two ceremonies. He wasn't very happy about it, for some reason. This was a man who'd drunk ayahuasca goodness knows how many times, maybe 40, 50 or 60 times. So he is obviously of the 'too much is never enough' point of view when it comes to spiritual psychedelics. Can even ayahuasca become a drug habit of sorts? Can you abuse plant medicine? #justasking

As for me, I stopped wearing a watch that day and stopped drinking alcohol completely so overall it was without doubt a profound, life-changing and positive experience. And yay, it's done so we get to have sex again!

THE END

A big thanks to everyone who told us they loved
Neanderthal Man.

Namaste!

☺

www.ingramcontent.com/pod-product-compliance
Lightning Source LLC
Chambersburg PA
CBHW020608030426
42337CB00013B/1280